# *Belonging*

Poems

Cherie Burbach

# *Belonging*

## Poems

### Cherie Burbach

Cherie Burbach

*Belonging*

Poems

Bonjour Publishing

All rights reserved.

Copyright © 2020 by Cherie Burbach

BELONGING

All rights reserved. No part of this book may be reproduced by mechanical, photographic, or electronic process, or in the form of a photographic recording; nor may it be stored in a retrieval system, transmitted, or otherwise be copied for public or private use - other than for "fair use" as brief quotations embodied in articles and reviews without prior written permission of the publisher.

Printed in the United States of America
978-0-9972274-8-2

*Belonging*

For
my husband

who has
shown me
the true
meaning of
belonging

Cherie Burbach

*Belonging*

# Also by Cherie Burbach

*Nonfiction*

Painting the Psalms
Art and Faith: Mixed Media Art
With a Faith-Filled Message
...and more

*Poetry*

Poiema
Angel Toughness
My Soul Is From a Different Place
Father's Eyes
The Difference Now
A New Dish
New and Selected Poems
Yes, You

Cherie Burbach

# Table of Contents

Table of Contents ............................................. 11

***Nearness*** .......................................................... 17

    *Perspective*............................................................ 19

    *I Show You My Shame* ........................................ 20

    *Wide Open*............................................................ 21

    *Walker Art Center Wind Chimes* ........................ 22

    *Doggies Speak*...................................................... 23

    *Selfish* .................................................................... 24

    *Finally Seen* .......................................................... 25

    *The Power of Art*.................................................. 26

    *It's Time* ................................................................ 27

    *Encourager*............................................................ 28

    *This Ache*.............................................................. 29

    *Gratitude* .............................................................. 30

    *Dreams Awakened*................................................ 31

    *Worth* .................................................................... 32

    *Graffiti* .................................................................. 33

    *Tea Party*.............................................................. 34

    *Shawl of Expectation* ............................................ 35

    *Bus Ticket*............................................................ 36

    *To Belong*.............................................................. 37

**Kinship** ............................................................. *41*
   *The Unwanted Child* ........................................ *43*
   *Inclusive* ............................................................. *45*
   *Right, Daddy?* .................................................... *48*
   *Our Voice* ........................................................... *51*
   *Your Age* ............................................................. *54*
   *Arrogant Blessings* .............................................. *56*
   *Hanging By a Thread (Unraveled)* ................... *58*
   *Her Biggest Fear* ................................................ *60*
   *What Loving Families Do* ................................. *61*
   *A Life* ................................................................. *64*
   *Not the Blessing* ................................................ *66*
   *How We Bury Our Dead* .................................. *68*
   *Lost In a Department Store* .............................. *70*
   *Gossip* ................................................................ *71*
   *Your Enduring Legacy* ...................................... *75*
   *Understand* ........................................................ *77*
   *I Was Yours, Too* .............................................. *80*

**Everlasting** ...................................................... *85*
   *Where She Belonged* ......................................... *87*
   *True Love* ........................................................... *88*
   *His Example Lost On You* ................................ *89*
   *His Way* .............................................................. *90*
   *Smiling Back* ..................................................... *92*

*Sunrise* ............................................. *93*

*I'll Keep On* ...................................... *95*

*He Will* ............................................. *97*

*Forgiveness Prayer* ............................. *98*

*He Is Good* ........................................ *99*

*Forever* ............................................. *100*

*The Garden* ...................................... *102*

About the Author ............................103

Cherie Burbach

# *Nearness*

# Perspective

Sometimes

we ask God
why

when
the words

we should
simply say are

"thank you."

Cherie Burbach

# I Show You My Shame

I lay out my shame
as a matter of fact.
It doesn't bind me
or limit me

but is
a long ago boundary
I learned
to redefine.

It's as boring
as the color of my hair
or what
I wore yesterday.

It's like looking
at photographs
of yourself
before you learned to smile.

I lay out my shame
so you can see
that happiness can grow
from even the darkest places.

# Wide Open

She let her heart break
wide open,

so there would be
more room

for God's grace
to fill the empty space.

## Walker Art Center Wind Chimes

A single chime
clangs against my bones

they struggle
against each other
like children fighting.

But the sculpture garden chimes
abundant in number
are a symphony
that calms
the soul.

Unity.

*Belonging*

# Doggies Speak

Doggies
were a
special part
of her world,

who spoke to her
with their
own language

but nevertheless,
had much
to say.

## Selfish

We
run
fastest

toward
the
ones
who
leave
us
behind

rather
than
the
loyal
friends

who
need
us
most.

# Finally Seen

Her hair was thin
her waist was thick
and her body and face
carried each painful memory
along with her happy moments.

Each made up
the person
she was now,

and although
some claimed
that she looked different,

she felt as if people
could finally see
her now.

# The Power of Art

Art speaks to us
in ways

we cannot answer
with words.

# It's Time

I guess
the only question

is what did you do
before I was
the scapegoat
for every one
of your
problems?

What did you do
when you had to
admit the problem
was you
and not
everyone else?

Oh honey,
have you
ever
done
that?

# Encourager

She was
an encourager.

Even though
she, too,
had grief
that she carried.

# This Ache

No, it doesn't help when you tell me about the pain
you went through when you had your children as
you then run off to play with your grandchildren.

I know you mean well.
I know you think it bonds us,

but it doesn't

because you have no idea what it's like to go through
this pain without the gift of life on the other side.
You have no idea what it's like to live with this ache,
each moment, from years before I knew until
the last moments of my breath.

# Gratitude

She scattered
gratitude

like
seeds

in a
garden.

# Dreams Awakened

Softly
a deep breath
released her worries.

Her sharp eyes
smiled
at dreams
awakened.

She was a woman
who loved
God.

# Worth

She knew her worth
she knew her value
she knew she was
enough.

She knew
she was
loved by Him.

# Graffiti

The gaggle
of gossipers
gorging on
my grief

their grotesque
gluttony
greedy
for my pain,

gobbling
down my
tears,

their attacks
like graffiti
on my
heart.

# Tea Party

You drank in
the tea I served,
along with the kindness
I offered,

sipping at first,
then slurping
it down greedily,
until you were full.

You grabbed
the tablecloth,
pulling and pulling,

while my own needs
for friendship
clamored to the floor
along with the dishes,
breaking into pieces,
one by one.

I cut myself
on the broken edges,
trying to clean up
the mess you left,
as you get up
barely glancing
down at me
there at your feet,
and walk away.

# Shawl of Expectation

You create a shawl of expectation
and place it around me
as if this should keep me warm.
You don't see that it is filled with holes
and even if I stand in the sun
the shawl provides no warmth.

And I do stand in the sun now.

God calls me there
when I am feeling low
and wondering why
you all can't just love me
as one of yours.

He beckons me toward Him,
removes the useless
shawl of expectation
and warms me through to my soul.

## Bus Ticket

When you've slept,
had enough to eat,
watch a little TV,
found yourself bored,
and rested again,

then your apology
to me comes,
when you finally
open your eyes
and see that I've
been here all along,
still crying from
your insensitivity
still reeling from
your neglect.

But by then
your apology is
too late,
like a ticket
for a bus
that has
already passed.

# To Belong

All we want is for someone
to want to get to know us
because we're human
and all humans deserve at least that.

All we want is to get
the benefit of the doubt.
So when someone hears a rumor
they shut it down,
no gossip on their watch,
especially because they
consider you a friend.

All we want is to be invited,
to have someone say,
*hey, we'd love to have you join us!*,
and mean it.

All we long for is kindness.
For those blessed with a support system
to remember us right away because
they know we're alone and they'd
never want us to stay that way.

All we wish for are holidays
that aren't filled with sadness,
because we always have people
we consider family
and a place we consider home.

Cherie Burbach

All we want is to be welcomed in
to that new group, with people
who make you feel like
they're glad you're there,
and not like you're the
butt of every joke.

All we wish for is that one person
who will share with us the
inside jokes in a way that
makes us feel as if
we've known them all along.

All we wish is for that person
who won't run to everyone else
before they come to you.

All we want is to be
surrounded with people who cherish us
because they know our heart,
and a relationship with us
is worth protecting.

All we want is for someone
to find out what things
have been like for us,
simply because they want
to understand.


All we want is to belong.

*Belonging*

# Kinship

Cherie Burbach

# The Unwanted Child

A child cannot
be both wanted
and given away.

Wanted children
are kept. Held.
Their birth,
celebrated,
not denied.

The wanted child
does not always arrive
when their parents plan.
And yet,
they are welcomed
into the world.
Parties are held
every year to celebrate
their birth by the people
who love them.

But the day
the unwanted child
enters the world
becomes a dark spot
in the life
of the one blessed
to birth them.

Cherie Burbach

Their birth is not
about new life,
but about the two people
who chose not to raise them.
And the memory of them
gets pushed away…

# Inclusive

Look, we've added your name
to our large family email list.
Attached you'll find pictures
from a dinner you weren't invited to.
Look how inclusive we are!
That is what family does!

And here, a story about
one of our family traditions.
You weren't there, of course,
but how dare you not remember!
Just because we didn't raise you
is no excuse for being different from us.

Why didn't you send me a birthday card!
I've missed your birthday 50 times
but we send cards in this family.
How could you be so thoughtless!

Okay, you wanted to be invited,
and because we are an inclusive family,
we very much want you to come to a
funeral, to honor someone you never met.
We will share memories so you can see
how much we've lived without you,
and we can watch you stand there alone
and ask each other why you're so odd.

Look, he goes to his mother's house for Holiday #1,
and she's different from your mother, of course,
so why would you even ask
if we wanted to spend the day with you?

## Cherie Burbach

How dare you make plans for Holiday #2!
Don't you know I had nothing to do!
I will tell everyone you didn't want to see me!
What is wrong with you?
What do you mean let's spend Holiday #3 together?
I demand to get together for Holiday #2!

Here's a picture from our
large family gathering for Holiday #3.
We knew you were alone and we didn't invite you,
but unlike you, I am inclusive
and that is why I'm forwarding this photo.
On behalf of *all* of us, Happy Holidays!

You must get to know the group at once!
That is what an inclusive family does!
What? You contacted a family member
on your own?
Without an introduction from me?
How dare you!
Now, compose an email to this next person
and give it to me so I can re-write it
and that way I will know every
move you make.
I will create drama between you two
before you've even met and then tell
you *there there*, get over it,
but if you see them on your own
and communicate directly
I will fly into a rage and ask
WHAT'S WRONG WITH YOU?

## Belonging

Hello darling, you've been quiet.
I have manipulated others against you
and am feeling happy now,
more at peace.
They do what I want.
It doesn't matter what the truth is.
Is there something wrong?
I haven't heard from you lately.

You will come to the next party
because I spent all this time
poisoning the well against you
and I want you there when you stand
five feet in front of me
and I cry to someone about you
hating me for no reason.
*I don't know what I ever did to her!*
You have to be there, darling.
I am inclusive!

# Right, Daddy?

Get over it!
he screamed
as he rallied
his enablers
for insulation
against the
consequences of
his actions.

What's wrong
with you!
they bellowed
so what
if he
left you
behind! So
what that
you weren't
loved! Let
us tell
you about
our family
stories, so
you can
see how
we continued
to live
without you,
because it
didn't matter.

*Belonging*

Get over it!
he screamed
again, when
I tried to
answer his
questions
about my
life. That's
not how I
want you
to be!
You're supposed
to adore me!
I want you
to be a
bubbly little girl!
Not a woman
who doesn't
know me
because I
walked away!
How sad
that you
won't do
everything
I want!

What's wrong
with her!
he cried to
his enablers,
the ones
he chose
to raise
instead of
leave behind.

Bad daughter!
they chimed.
Right, Daddy?
We want you
to love us,
so bad, bad, bad,
she's bad,
not like me,
right, Daddy?
I don't want
to feel guilty
when you die,
so I'll say
what you want!
That's love,
right, Daddy?

# Our Voice

We don't have time
for your pain.

We don't dwell on things
like you do.

We are not emotional
like you are.

Can you please send us love?
Because we are sad today.

But our sadness is real,
not like yours.

You have to
get over all that.

We don't dwell on things
like you do.

But look at this picture
from our past.

See how we all had
each other?

You must have had people,
too? No?

Cherie Burbach

We don't have time
for complaints!
We are strong people,
not like you.

Can you send us
good wishes today?

We have reality on our doorstep
and it is too much.

If we were people
who complained,

we would say more,
but we aren't, not like you.

Our eyes brim with tears
but we are not emotional.

We can't imagine
being emotional like you.

Why are you
talking about yourself!

You only read eleven of our
twelve emails!

How dare you
talk about your past!

We never do that!
Which reminds us,

*Belonging*

when we were five,
we had something happen,

which happens to everyone,
but let us explain

because the sounds of
our voice is pleasing to us.

## Your Age

I am your age now,
the last year
you breathed air.
The last time
you had the chance
to atone for your ways
and instead held
tight to the
control you thought
you had.

You said your age
made you wise.
Made you *right*.
Your age justified
the things you did.
The life-long threats
you gave me
to remain quiet
were because your age
meant you knew
better than me.

*Belonging*

And yet, I'm
your age now,
and I can see how
much you lied.
I can see that the
pain you caused
never should
have happened.
I can see that
you weren't smart,
you were not kind,
you were childish,
your actions, evil.

If I could look you
in the eye today,
adult to adult,
I would tell you
to grow up,
stop whining,
stop bullying me,
and act your age.

## Arrogant Blessings

You had a family
who loved you
caring parents
brothers and sisters
and nieces and nephews
and kids of your own.

You look at those
around you who lack
these blessings and
think somehow they
must not have tried
hard enough,

it's their fault
they're alone
and you say
*we'll get together soon*
because it makes
you feel good

to say it, but even
as the words come
out of your mouth,
you're calling up
your tribe instead,
the ones who have
blessings just like you

*Belonging*

because why should
you worry about
the ones alone
and hurting?

You *told* them
you think of
them as family.
Wasn't that enough?

# Hanging By a Thread (Unraveled)

Did you know I was
hanging by a thread?

Grasping the fabric
of your family
hanging on
so you wouldn't
forget me.

You tried to cut this string
an annoyance
something you thought
didn't belong

something you thought
detracted from the overall
fabric of
your family garment.

I kept pulling,
silently,
before you even knew
I existed,
before you even remembered
I was once a part of the whole,
or at least,
I was supposed to be

*Belonging*

but you thought
I didn't fit,
I was a skipped stitch,
a hiccup on the
creation machine.

Every few years
you swiped at your sleeve
absentmindedly,
while I, miles and years away,
clung to the thought that
I could be made part of the family whole,
knitted together
with the rest of the group.

But you pushed me away,
while the thread
slipped through my fingers
while I desperately tried
to prevent the unraveling

and while you tucked me
into your sleeve
like something you could hide,
like something you don't want
to take care of right now,
like something you could

weave in at some point,
or cut loose,
it didn't matter,
as long as you looked good.

# Her Biggest Fear

Her biggest fear
was not looking at that little girl's face
and seeing a soul ripped in two,

one half by the violence
her body had learned
to brace itself for

and one half by the words
that would circle
around her head

like a prickly crown
made from roses,
the blossoms

a beautiful image
but underneath them
thorns scratching her skin.

No,
her biggest fear
was losing him.

If her home
didn't have
a man,

how could
she smile
in the morning?

*Belonging*

# What Loving Families Do

They scream at her
because she's not like them,
tell lies about what she did or didn't do,
and cluck their tongues in disgust
after they tell her exactly
what they think of her.

*What's wrong with her*, they say,
feeling smug
that they've admonished
the woman
who found them.

How dare she arrive
after half a century of them
pretending that her
life didn't matter.

They ignore her,
run from her affection,
make fun of her painful past,
and then give her a command
about showing up at an event
and playing dutiful daughter.

*That's what families do!*,
they add,
for good measure.

The more they can
list the faults they see
in her, the better they
feel about leaving
her behind.

But loving families
don't treat her
as they have.

Loving families
take responsibility
for their actions,
apologize when
they behave poorly,
treat everyone with care
and kindness.

Loving families
don't reward liars
and manipulators.
They don't
make up stories
to pit one member
against another.

And they don't
bury their heads
in the sand
when the new person
is being picked on
and targeted.

Loving families
don't leave
children behind.

*Belonging*

Loving families
don't treat
those children
who grow up
without them
as if it was
their fault
they were
given away.

# A Life

She wanted to feel love,
or something good,
or just nothing.
He seemed smart, intelligent,
she let him,
so quick, the door slams,
and he's gone.
On to the next
bit of fun.

She tells him,
he gives her money.
Do what you want;
I won't judge,
I'm religious so
whatever she does it
can't be on
my conscience.

She shows up again,
she gave it away,
but wants him to know.
He needs to just know,
and by the way,
it was a girl.

A girl! He would have
liked that! Oh well,
maybe he'll have another
some day and this time,
he'll raise it.

*Belonging*

Half a century,
and she wants
the girl to know why,
and he wants the girl
to help him,
but oh girl,
we don't care
about what's
happened to you!
Don't whine
about your life,
but listen to ours!
It's about us,
it always was,
can't you see that?

# Not the Blessing

She felt,
not the blessing
of this life
growing
inside her

but the shame
society placed
on her.

As the heartbeat
gained strength,
so did
her dismay.

The pain
of lost choices
if she raised
a baby alone

what if she
never married
after that?

No, being
without a man
was the
one thing
she couldn't
risk her
future on.

*Belonging*

So she
gave
away
her blessing.

# How We Bury Our Dead

This is how
we bury our dead
she says,
and tells me that is is
proper to stand before
the casket of someone
I never met,
and now, never will,
and honor their life.

Make sure
he's happy
she says,
of the man
who abandoned me
and fifty years later
doesn't want to
hear about
my life.

He screams and lies
and manipulates
because if you don't
make him happy
you'll regret it.

Look at
your brother,
she says,
he does
what daddy wants
even if he knows
it is wrong.
He'll attack you

*Belonging*

because then
Daddy will
be happy
and brother
will feel good
about himself
when Daddy dies.

And I wonder
how they
don't see
that the way
to truly
honor life
is to
treat it
with respect
and kindness
while we are
here, alive.

## Lost In a Department Store

She searched them out
like a child
lost in a department store
feeling somehow
it was her fault,
as if she had dropped
her mommy's hand
for a moment
and had to run from
aisle to aisle
to find her.

She foolishly thought
they'd be searching, too,
like a frantic parent,
scanning the aisles
for their child,
praying fervently
that she was okay,
that they'd find her,
and take her home.

She found them at last,
not caring that she'd been gone,
not wanting to know
if she was okay,
instead enjoying all the things
they brought home
without her,
like a shopper on Christmas Eve,
filling their carts
with one child
after another.

# Gossip

You laugh, mock,
and thoroughly
enjoy yourself.
She deserves it,
you reason.
She supposedly did
this and that and this
because that's
what you've heard
and what you didn't hear
you made up,
but you like to call it
embellishing.

And so what,
she's not perfect,
so why not blame her,
I mean, really,
things changed after
she arrived
so it must be
totally her fault.
Right?

A word here,
a story there,
a snide remark
followed by a
nasty smirk,
it all makes you
feel good
to have a focus
for your hate

and pet peeves,
and irritation
that the world
never stays the same.

But at the end of
each word that
leaves your mouth

is
a
real
live
person

who doesn't deserve
your gossip and
who grieves the
losses life has
given her.

This
real
live
person

doesn't even
know you,
nor you her,
but you create
a narrative
about her.

*Belonging*

It makes you
feel justified
that your words
aren't really
all that mean
or wrong
or misconstrued
or entirely false,

but
this
real
live
person

hears them
anyway, and
they hurt her,
as you wanted
them to do,

and she cries
about the
lack of respect
and that brings
you joy as well

and one day
your lies
will be exposed
but it might
not be
this side of heaven.

Until then,
you stalk her,
look her up
and call up
the "gang" to
share in
your disgust
of all she does
and all you think
she is.

You never
want to know
who she
really is
because then
you'll feel bad
about kicking
around someone
who didn't deserve
your hate

and we can't
have that
because better
blame her
than yourself

and you never
think that just
like you
she is

a
real
live
person.

# Your Enduring Legacy

You were blessed
with family who love you,
a life without want,
so when I came into
your world it was just
another thing you thought
you deserved.

You accepted my love
like overdue rain,

arms out
to catch
every drop,

mouth open
to taste
the goodness,

eyes closed
to feel it seep
into your skin.

And I was happy
to pour my love
over you,
until I was empty
and had nothing
left to give.

But one day,
I needed kindness,
a simple moment
of understanding,
and you cut me
through like a
bitter wind.

Having to give
love was something
you were never
taught, and your
enduring legacy
will be teaching
your selfishness
to the next
generation.

# Understand

I wondered
how a man could leave a child behind,
his child, and then deny it was ever his,
and then say he just didn't have time,
that it was inconvenient,
that it's just how it was in those days,
you understand, right?

And I said, sure, I get it,
what's in the past is in the past.
Sure, I understand.

But I didn't.

I wondered
how, when he met me, a half century later,
he didn't care that he'd left me
with a single mother
who would follow in his footsteps.
No time for me, she wanted to find a man
and if she had a kid she couldn't find a man
and you understand, she said, right?

And I said, sure, it must have been hard.
Sure, who blame you?
Sure, I understand.

But I didn't.

I wondered
how a woman could decided
that a man was more important
than her child, how once she got her man,
well then she wished she hadn't given me away,
how she said it was just bad timing. Again.
And and she asked me,
you understand, right, I had no choice?

And I said, sure, okay, yeah…
I understand.

But I didn't.

And I asked her about him,
and him about her,
and I tried to understand how they
didn't know each other,
how they could share their bodies
but not their love.

And I said, yeah, it happens.
I get it.

But I didn't.

*Belonging*

Because I wasn't blessed
with so many children
I could leave a few behind,
and I didn't understand how you
could put your hands up in protest,
saying hey, not my fault,
when I lived the consequences
of your actions
with abusive parents
and people who told me
I was worthless, because in the end
I was never really considered theirs.

No, I didn't understand that at all.

If I had understood,
I'd be just like you,
so I was glad that I didn't.

# I Was Yours, Too

You refer to me as his daughter,
not His daughter,
not a child of God,
but of him,
your brother and father and nephew and uncle.

You get to know me so you can report to him.
He bellows displeasure at yet another thing
the daughter he gave away did or failed to do,
the daughter he never knew
as a baby or little girl or young woman,
the one he met after a half century,

and you run to me and tell me
how awful it is that he is unhappy.

You tell me,
call him, text him,
do what he wants you to do,
and I do.

And even then,
he is unhappy.

*Belonging*

And you tell me,
do more,
call him more,
call him less,
don't give him gifts,
do give him gifts,
invite him for the holidays,
why did you invite him!
he feels bad!
why did you make him feel bad!

As he screams at me,
temper tantrums that demonstrate
the man who lost jobs and wives and money,
and me.

You remind me again and again and again,
he's your father,
this man I met a handful of times,
who lied and manipulated and pretended
with the skill of an award winning actor.
He lamented "what did I ever do to her" right after
he called me names and told me he thought of me
as a girlfriend, almost, hee hee, kinda,
and also, this other gal is really who should be my
daughter,
not you,
but what is your problem!

And you all believed him.
You all consoled him,
took up his mission
to lament "what's wrong with her"
even though if you just opened
your eyes and ears and heart
you would know.

You'd know why I pulled away
like a child backhanded for
doing nothing more than being born
when it wasn't convenient.
You'd know why I said
my heart was broken.
You'd know
how unwanted I felt… again.

Because I wasn't just his daughter.
I was your niece.
I was your cousin.
I was your sister.
I was part of your genes,
part of your history.

I was yours, as much as his.
I was yours, too.

# *Everlasting*

Cherie Burbach

*Belonging*

# Where She Belonged

She searched
her whole life

for the people
who would

welcome her
as family

and finally
found home

in the
embrace

of the one
she loved.

# True Love

To fill her life with flowers
would be as much like heaven
to her as spending eternity
with everyone who had
ever loved her,

who had ever seen her
for who she was
and loved her faithful heart.

How wonderful the fragrance
of true love.

*Belonging*

# His Example Lost On You

You ask why I cry,
and tell me that
God is here for me.

You go off on your own,
leave me again,
and remind me that
God will be here for me.

And as I say
I know all that,
you are gone again.

God will always
be here for me,
I know that.

But sometimes
I wish you
could show me
the compassion
He taught.

# His Way

Lord,
take away my loneliness.
Give it to the one
who you've blessed so much
they mocked me, saying
they were just too busy
to be lonely.
They'll never understand
unless they experience
it as I have.

Lord,
take away my childlessness.
Give it to the one
who has kids but complains
that they can't have more.
They use the word infertility
to describe their pain,
but they'll never understand
what that means until
they go through it
as I have.

Lord,
take away my self-doubt.
Give it to the one
who uses it to get
attention from me,
keeping me just out of reach
of real love. Help them
to see the damage they do
with their emotional games.
Let them feel the confusion
as I have.

Lord,
take away my ideas
of justice and life.
Give them to the one
who replaces every good thing
you do with a poor substitute.
Show him that your love
and your justice are
the only thing real.
And then take me
to your world,
where I can
finally be free.

## Smiling Back

My smile
is genuine

because the
joy inside me

is from
God.

When you
find yourself

smiling back
it is the

goodness
of grace

that pulls at
the corners

of your
lips

until you
can't help

but feel
the gift

of
His love.

# Sunrise

You wake me early
before the sunrise,
when the world is
filled with darkness.
I am troubled
with tears rolling
down my face.
I long for the sun to rise.

I am angry, at you,
at injustice, at a world
in which some seem
to have everything,
with others have
nothing at all.
I long for the sun to rise.

My heart grieves,
and I ask you where you are.
I ache for an answer,
to hear your voice,
but the birds chirping
in the darkness
are all I hear in return.

I long for the sun to rise
so the new day can begin,
so light can lift me
from this nightly grief.

I long for the sun to rise,
I long for the sun to rise,
for the sun to rise,
for the Son to rise.

# I'll Keep On

I'll keep on talking
about how you hurt me
because it is God
that gives me strength
to forgive you.

I'll keep on crying
without shame at the
grief I carry daily
because it is God
that comforts me.

I'll keep on admitting
that I'm afraid
because it is God
that gives me courage
to fight another day.

I'll keep on writing
about injustice
because it is God
that will decide right and wrong
in the end.

I'll keep on painting
my unanswered dreams
because it is God
that will bring me
home one day.

I'll keep on praying
through His silence
because it is God
that will give
and take away.

I'll keep on.
I'll keep on.
I'll keep on.

# He Will

"This burden is so heavy," she said,
pointing to her heart
that ached with bad memories.

"Can you take some of it for me?"
she asked, but I had learned
that each time I held her pain,

the weight of it grew and grew.

"I can't take it from you,"
I said, as I prayed for God
to lift it from her instead.

"Only He can do that.
But the good part is that
He will."

Cherie Burbach

# Forgiveness Prayer

I forgive you,
she said,

although she
didn't feel it.

I forgive you,
she prayed,

to help
make it true.

# He Is Good

I ask God to shed His grace on you,
not because I am good,
but because He is.

You roll your eyes,
don't believe me,
go back to gossiping
about me and spreading lies
that hurt, because I am human
and mistreatment, even by people
I can no longer call friends, hurts.

I ask Him to help me with that hurt,
and to help me forgive you,
and I ask Him to forgive you, too.
And then I ask Him to forgive me,
for every time I made a situation
worse, rather than turning the other cheek,
for every time I hurt someone else
the way you hurt me.

I ask God to shed His grace on you,
not because I am good,
but because He is.

# Forever

He says, "Come here, sit,"
and pats the space beside him.
I sit. Yes?
"I love you," he says, the words
running through to my soul,
and yet, my response
was simply, "I know."

I say, "She couldn't keep me,"
and tell him that
I'm running off to find her.
"She must be lost without me."

He frowns and pulls
at my arm as I run away,
determined to find her.

I seek him out later for comfort,
tears streaming down my face.
I ask him why, again and again.
"She didn't want me!" I scream
at him, angry and hurt.

He smiles at me.
"I love you," he says,
but even then I wonder
why she didn't.

"Stay with me," he says,
but I'm off again,
chasing after someone else,
the one who walked away.
"I was a baby, he couldn't
have known that I'd grow up

and need him," I say,
words tumbling out fast
as I open the door to go.

I hear a faint,
"I love you" again,
as I run, far and fast,
to the one who left.

When I come back again,
my anger is blinding.
I scream at Him,
"Why did you do this?
Why did you give me
to a family who didn't
want me!"

And he says, "I didn't."
And again, I remind him
of being given away,
being raised by people
who mistreated me,
and then trying to find
the family of my birth,
only to have them
treat me like anything
but family.

And he holds my hand, and says,
"I love you so much
I died so you could
be with me forever."
And finally, I feel like
I belong.

# The Garden

She planted
her sadness

in the field
of her faith,

so God could
water each

dreary thought
with His love

and transform
it into hope.

# About the Author

Cherie Burbach is a poet, freelance writer, and mixed media artist.

She uses book pages, Bible verses, music sheets, and other random things in her art to create a hopeful, faith-filled message.

For more on Cherie, visit her website, cherieburbach.com.

www.ingramcontent.com/pod-product-compliance
Lightning Source LLC
Chambersburg PA
CBHW070435010526
44118CB00014B/2054